P9-DGL-947

Make Every Day Beautiful

A Collection of
INSPIRATION & BEAUTY

FALL
RIVER
PRESS
New York

FALL RIVER PRESS

New York

An Imprint of Sterling Publishing Co., Inc.
1166 Avenue of the Americas
New York, NY 10036

FALL RIVER PRESS and the distinctive Fall River Press logo are registered trademarks of Barnes & Noble Booksellers, Inc.

Cover and interior design, compilation © 2018 Tandem Books, Inc.

All rights reserved. No part of this publication may be reproduced, stored in a retrieval system, or transmitted in any form or by any means (including electronic, mechanical, photocopying, recording, or otherwise) without prior written permission from the publisher.

Any trademarks are the property of their respective owners, are used for editorial purposes only, and the publisher makes no claim of ownership and shall acquire no right, title, or interest in such trademarks by virtue of this publication.

ISBN 978-1-4351-6818-3

For information about custom editions, special sales, and premium and corporate purchases, please contact Sterling Special Sales at 800-805-5489 or specialsales@sterlingpublishing.com.

Manufactured in China

2 4 6 8 10 9 7 5 3 1

sterlingpublishing.com

Front cover image © LazarenkoD/Shutterstock.com
Back cover image © Cegli/Shutterstock.com
Endpapers image © bbearlyam/Shutterstock.com
Image Credits—See Last Page

MAKE EVERY DAY BEAUTIFUL!

What if every day was a beautiful one? What if every time you woke up, the sun was shining, flowers were blooming, and you just knew it was going to be one of those magical days when everything goes your way? While you can't control the weather and the seasons, you can control that sense of beauty. You can have that confidence that this day is *your* day. Because, whether you realize it or not, a beautiful day has everything to do with your attitude. If you *know* it's going to be a gorgeous day, even storm clouds will be stunning. Raindrops will throw off rainbows. Cold winds will make your home a comforting beacon.

Make Every Day Beautiful is a collection of quotes, wisdom, and truisms that will remind you how truly beautiful each day is, and how lucky you are to be living in this crazy world. Couple these maxims with amazing photography, and you get powerful reminders to live your best life, find your bliss, and even just forget the dirty dishes and dance!

Let these quotes from across the ages and images from around the world inspire you, ignite your passion, and comfort you. But most of all, let them keep your eyes open to the beauty that is around you—and in you —each and every day.

LET US MAKE
OUR FUTURE NOW,
AND LET US MAKE
OUR DREAMS
TOMORROW'S REALITY.

—MALALA YOUSAFZAI

H.O.P.E.
(Hold on! Pain Ends.)

Strive for progress, not perfection.

She turned her can'ts
into cans and her
dreams into plans.

-Kobi Yamada

BE A FOUNTAIN,
NOT A DRAIN.

THERE IS ALWAYS SOMETHING TO CELEBRATE!

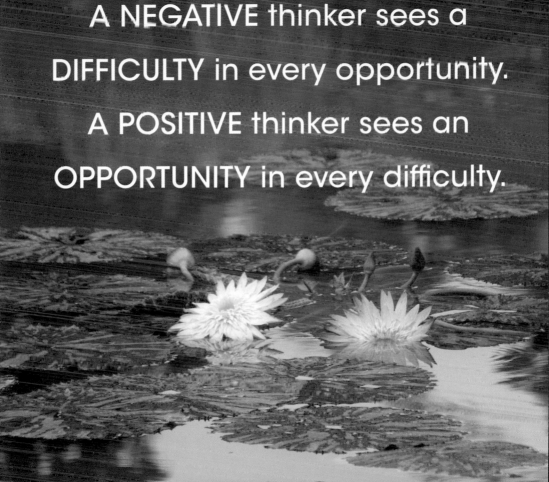

There are flowers
everywhere for
those who want
to see them.

−Henri Matisse

LIFE HAS GOT ALL THOSE TWISTS AND TURNS. YOU'VE GOT TO HOLD ON TIGHT AND OFF YOU GO.

—NICOLE KIDMAN

PATIENCE IS A BITTER PLANT,
BUT IT HAS SWEET FRUIT.

-PROVERB

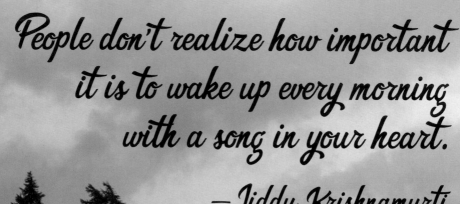

People don't realize how important it is to wake up every morning with a song in your heart.

—Jiddu Krishnamurti

Joy is the best wine.

−George Eliot

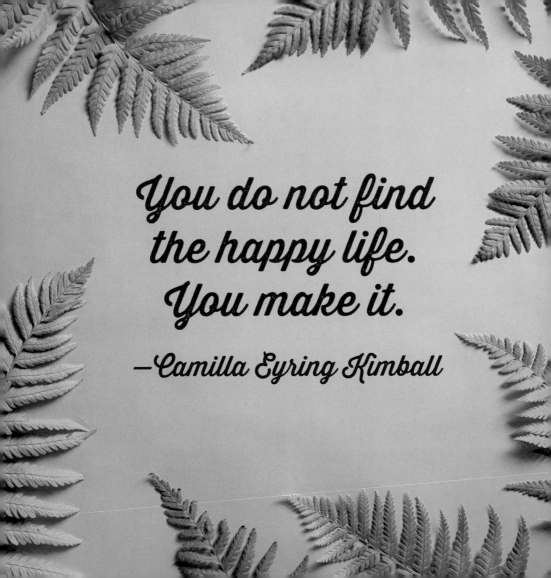

You do not find the happy life. You make it.

—Camilla Eyring Kimball

And all the loveliest things there be
Come simply, so it seems to me.

—Edna St. Vincent Millay

Though we travel the world over to find the beautiful, we must carry it with us or we find it not.

—Ralph Waldo Emerson

A good heart is better than all the heads in the world.

—Edward Bulwer-Lytton

Protect your magic.

TODAY ME WILL LIVE IN THE MOMENT UNLESS IT'S UNPLEASANT IN WHICH CASE ME WILL EAT A COOKIE.

—COOKIE MONSTER

What is joy? A sunbeam between two clouds.

—Madame Deluzy

LIVE WELL.

LAUGH OFTEN.

LOVE MUCH.

The best is yet
to come . . .

If you look at
what you have
in life, you'll always
have more.

—Oprah Winfrey

Don't wait.
The time
will never be
just right.

—Napoleon Hill

Exuberance
is beauty.

—William Blake

Oh, the places you'll go!
-Dr. Seuss

You are never too old to set another goal or to dream a new dream.

-C. S. Lewis

IT ISN'T WHERE YOU CAME FROM. IT'S WHERE YOU'RE GOING THAT COUNTS.

—ELLA FITZGERALD

ENJOY THE RICH, THE EVER-LIVING BEAUTY!

—JOHANN WOLFGANG VON GOETHE

The most wasted of days
is one without laughter.

—e e cummings

If I cannot do great things, I can do small things in a great way.

—Martin Luther King, Jr.

THE BAD NEWS IS TIME FLIES. THE
GOOD NEWS IS YOU'RE THE PILOT.
—Michael Altshuler

Dare to live your dreams.

The greatest things in life are the people we love, the places we've been, and the memories made along the way.

Pie makes everybody happy.

—Laurie Halse Anderson

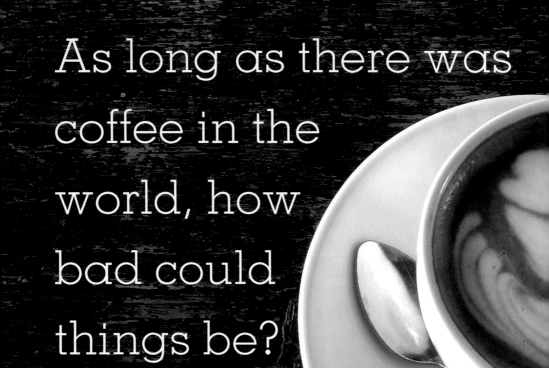

As long as there was coffee in the world, how bad could things be?

—Cassandra Clare

Joys are our wings,
sorrows our spurs.

-Jean Paul Richter

The beautiful attracts the beautiful.

—Leigh Hunt

THE FUTURE IS BRIGHT!

WILL YOUR WORRIES TODAY MATTER NEXT YEAR?

As you start to walk on the way, the way appears.

—Rumi

TO FLY YOU MUST FIRST LOVE YOURSELF

IF YOU STOP CHASING THE WRONG THINGS, THE RIGHT THINGS WILL HAVE A CHANCE TO CATCH YOU.

[We] can complain that rose bushes have thorns or rejoice that thorn bushes have roses.

—J. K. Morley

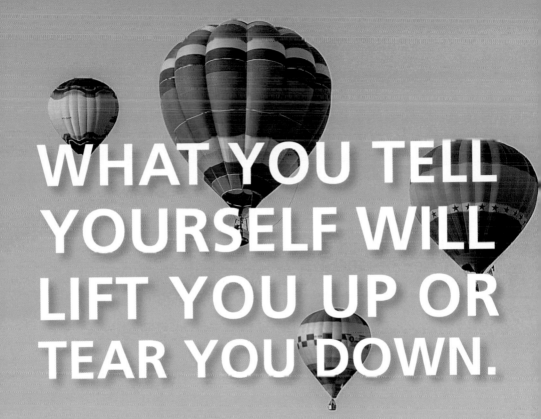

WHAT YOU TELL
YOURSELF WILL
LIFT YOU UP OR
TEAR YOU DOWN.

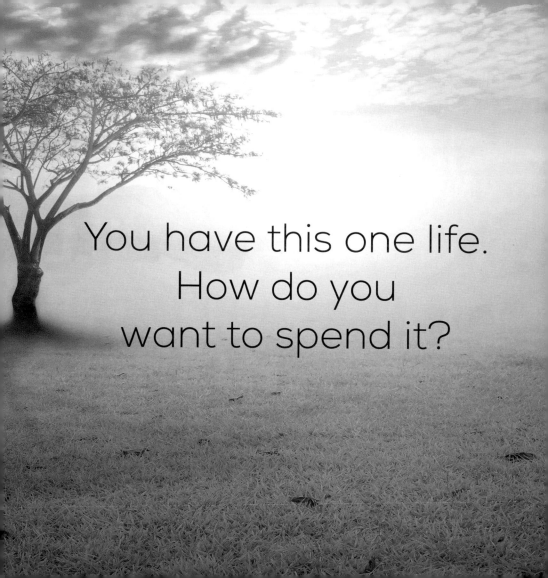

WORRY IS A WASTE OF A PERFECTLY GOOD IMAGINATION.

Treat yourself with
loving kindness.
If you are gentle
with yourself, you will
be gentle with others.

– Lama Thubten Yeshe

A positive attitude gives you power over your circumstances instead of your circumstances having power over you.

—Joyce Meyer

WE ARE MADE
OF STARSTUFF.
—CARL SAGAN

For every minute of anger, you lose sixty seconds of happiness.

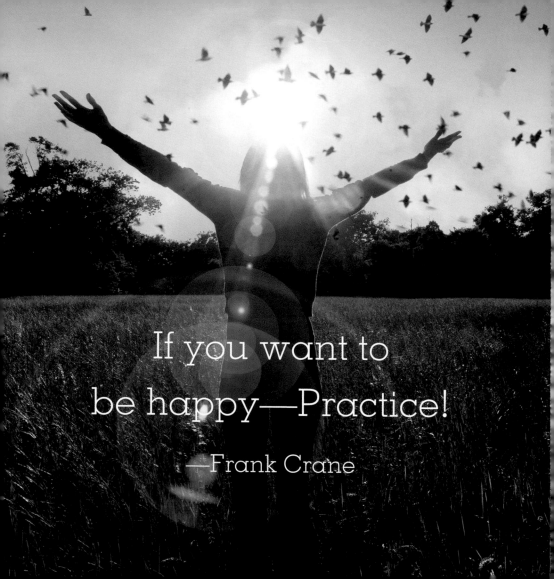

If you want to
be happy—Practice!

—Frank Crane

Happiness is when what you think, what you say, and what you do are in harmony.

FIND
YOUR
BLISS.

Happiness is not a goal,
it is a byproduct.

—Eleanor Roosevelt

Above all, be the heroine of your life, not the victim.

—Nora Ephron

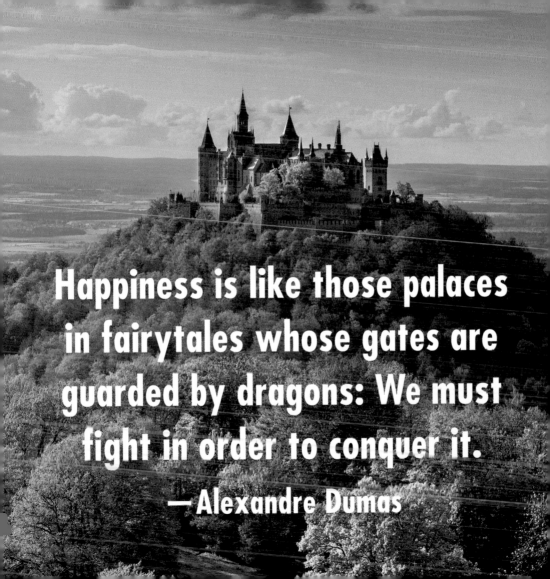

Happiness is like those palaces in fairytales whose gates are guarded by dragons: We must fight in order to conquer it.

—Alexandre Dumas

THE BEGINNING IS ALWAYS TODAY.

–MARY WOLLSTONECRAFT

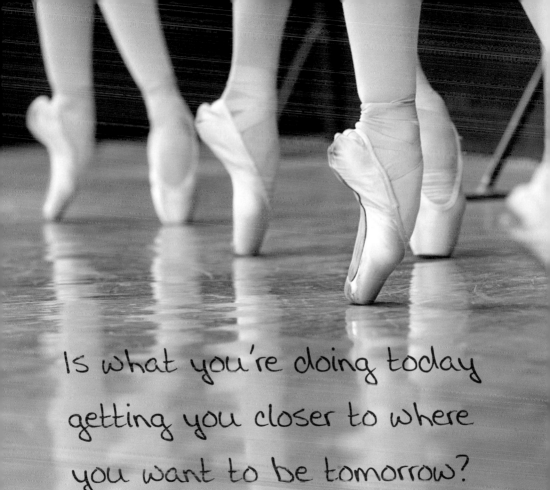

Is what you're doing today getting you closer to where you want to be tomorrow?

Every day we are engaged in a miracle which we don't even realize: a blue sky, white clouds, green leaves, the black, curious eyes of a child—our own two eyes. *All is a miracle.*

—Thich Nhat Hanh

Live in the sunshine, swim the sea, drink the wild air's salubrity.

--Ralph Waldo Emerson

KNOW THAT YOU CAN START OVER EACH AND EVERY MORNING.

Rules for Happiness.
Something to do, someone to love,
something to hope for.

—Immanuel Kant

IMPRESS
FUTURE
YOU.

A diamond is a chunk of coal that did well under pressure.

STAY LOW, STAY QUIET,
KEEP IT SIMPLE, DON'T
EXPECT TOO MUCH,
ENJOY WHAT YOU HAVE.

—DEAN KOONTZ

You are enough just
as you are.

–Meghan Markle

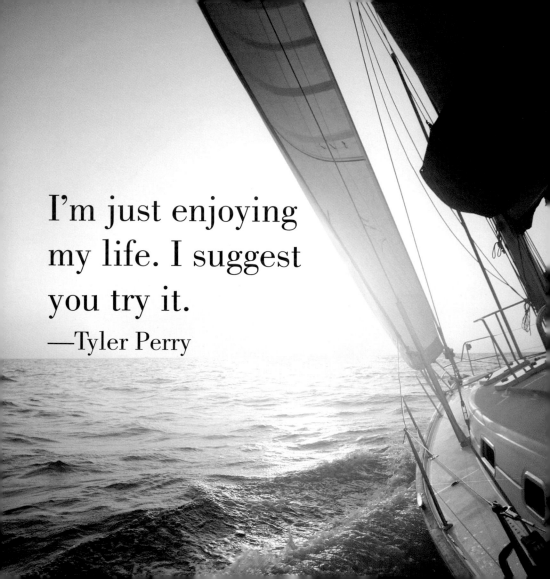

I'm just enjoying my life. I suggest you try it.

—Tyler Perry

GET OUT OF YOUR OWN WAY.

ONE OF THE SECRETS OF A HAPPY LIFE IS CONTINUOUS SMALL TREATS. —IRIS MURDOCH

Stop a moment,
cease your work,
look around you.

—Leo Tolstoy

TODAY SHOULD ALWAYS BE OUR MOST *WONDERFUL* DAY.

—THOMAS DREIER

You got this!

You are imperfect, permanently and inevitably flawed. And you are beautiful.

—Amy Bloom

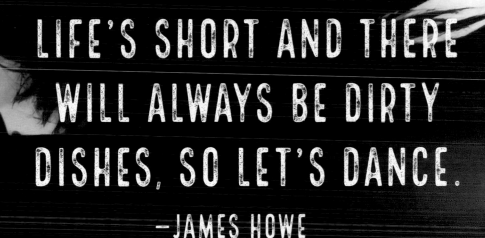

LIFE'S SHORT AND THERE WILL ALWAYS BE DIRTY DISHES, SO LET'S DANCE.

—JAMES HOWE

Dance till the stars come down with the rafters Dance, dance, dance till you drop.

—W. H. Auden

DEEP IN THEIR ROOTS,
ALL FLOWERS KEEP
THE LIGHT.

—Theodore Roethke

THE EYES ARE THE WINDOWS OF THE SOUL.

—OLD PROVERB

ALL PROFOUNDLY ORIGINAL WORK LOOKS UGLY AT FIRST.

-CLEMENT GREENBERG

Beauty is truth—
truth, beauty—
that is all ye know
on earth, and all ye
need to know.

—John Keats

You must lose a fly
to catch a trout.

—George Herbert

Now and then it's good to pause in our pursuit of happiness and just be happy.

—Guillaume Apollinaire

AS LONG AS WE LIVE,
THERE IS NEVER
ENOUGH SINGING.
—MARTIN LUTHER

One who wants a rose

must respect the thorn.

—Persian proverb

A day spent with dreaming and sunsets and refreshing breezes cannot be bettered.

—Nicholas Sparks

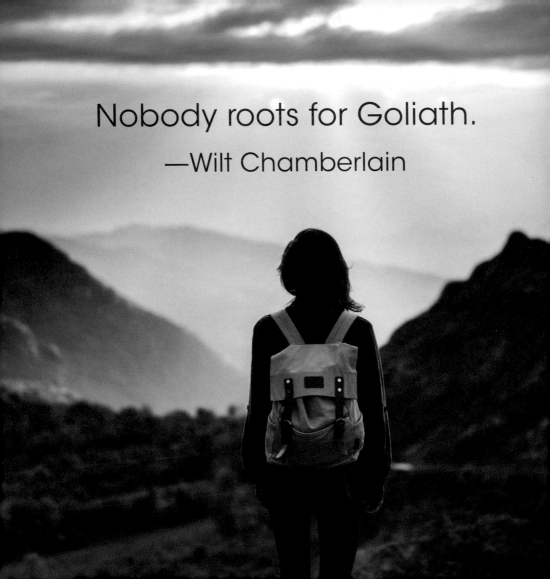

Nobody roots for Goliath.

—Wilt Chamberlain

Disappointments
should be cremated,
not embalmed.

—Henry S. Haskins

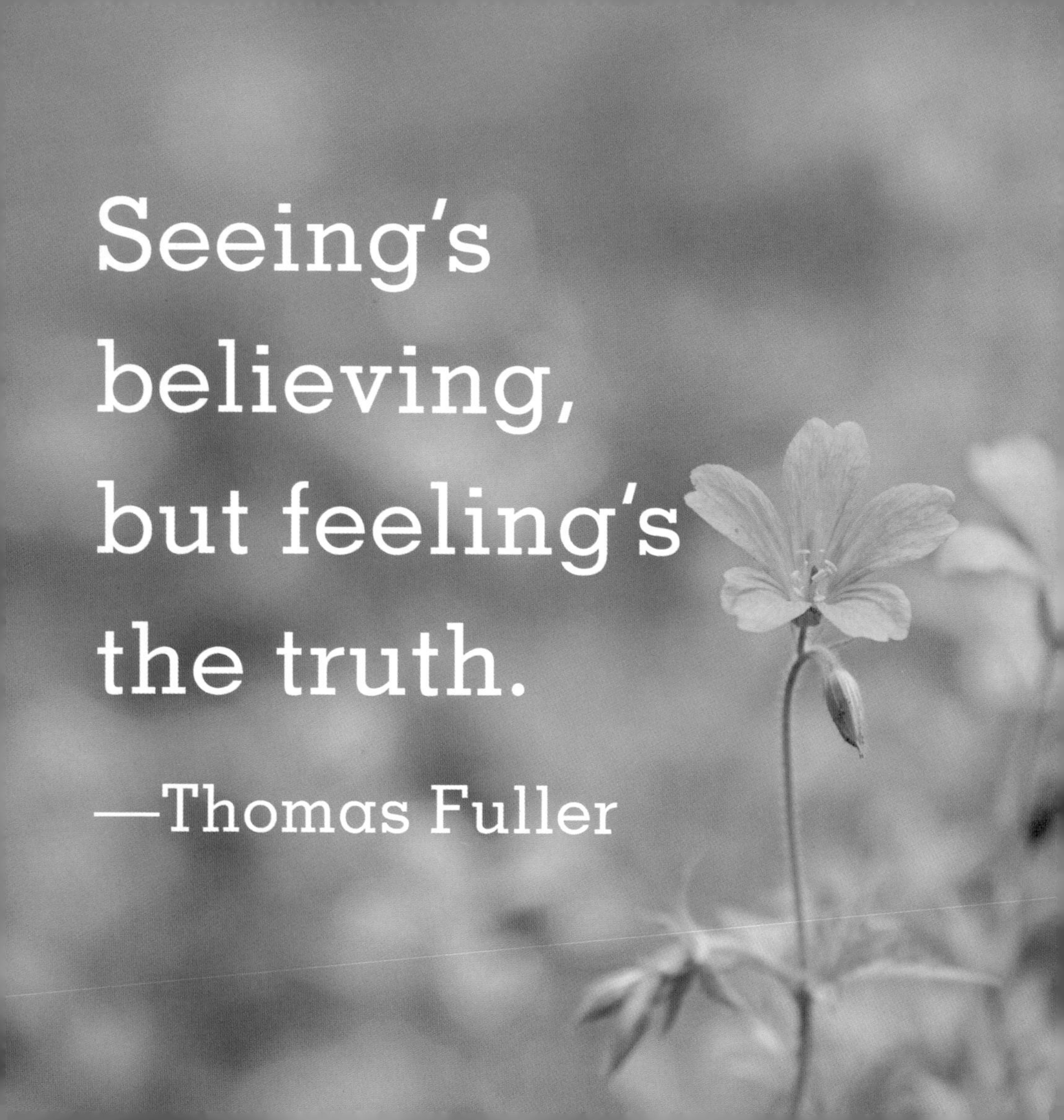

Seeing's
believing,
but feeling's
the truth.

—Thomas Fuller

PATIENCE AND PASSAGE OF TIME DO MORE THAN STRENGTH AND FURY.

—JEAN DE LA FONTAINE

You live once and life is wonderful, so eat the damned red velvet cupcake.
-Emma Stone

NEVER CUT WHAT YOU CAN UNTIE.

-JOSEPH JOUBERT

ANYTHING THAT COMES
EASY, COMES WRONG.

—JOSEPHINE TESSIER

WHY AREN'T YOU
DANCING WITH
JOY AT THIS
VERY MOMENT?

—VILAYAT INAYAT KHAN

Rosiness is not a worse windowpane than gloomy gray when viewing the world.

– Grace Paley

IN UPLIFTING,
GET UNDERNEATH.

—GEORGE ADE

NOTHING IS SO BURDENSOME AS A SECRET.

—FRENCH PROVERB

Listening means listening—not waiting for your turn to speak.

Macho does not prove mucho.

—Zsa Zsa Gabor

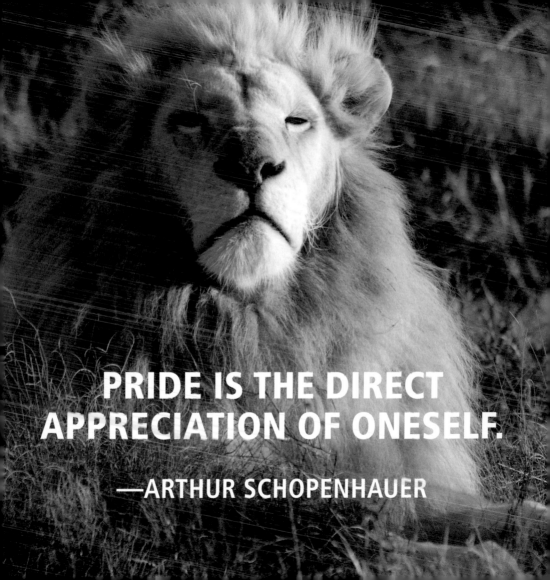

PRIDE IS THE DIRECT APPRECIATION OF ONESELF.

—ARTHUR SCHOPENHAUER

If you get tired,
learn to rest,
not quit.

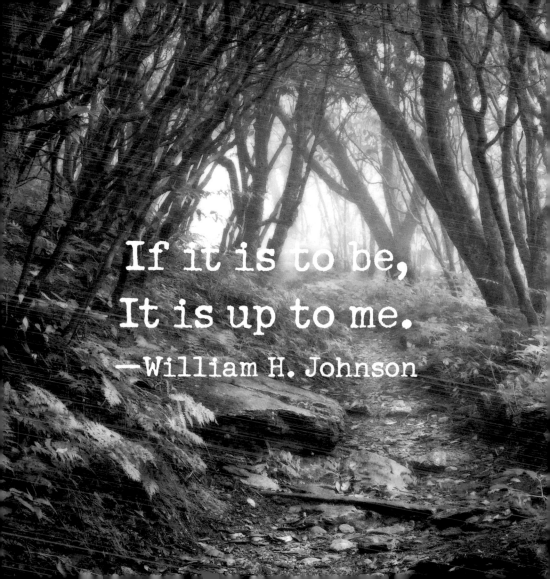

You are all you will
ever have for certain.

—June Havoc

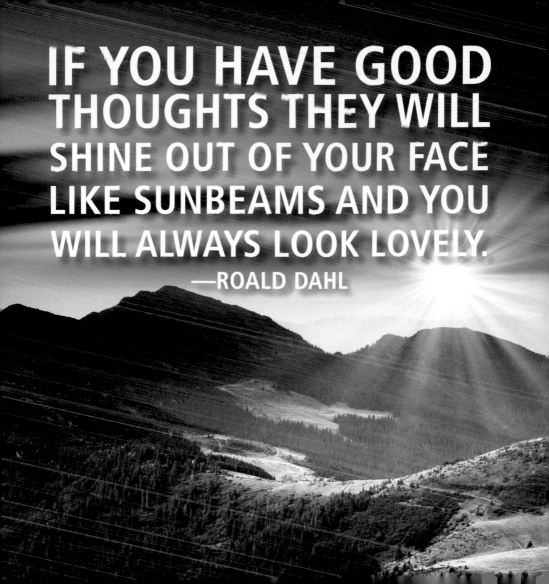

EVERY PATH HAS ITS PUDDLE.

—OLD SAYING

A HARD DAY'S WORK IS THE BEST PILLOW.

—HINDU PROVERB

ALL WOULD LIVE LONG, BUT NONE WOULD BE OLD.

—PROVERB

Nothing in human life . . . is ever right until it is beautiful.

—Harry Emerson Fosdick

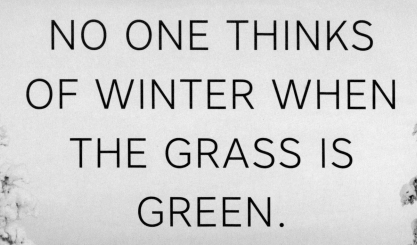

NO ONE THINKS
OF WINTER WHEN
THE GRASS IS
GREEN.

—RUDYARD KIPLING

No Winter lasts forever,
no Spring skips its turn.
—Hal Borland

No need to hurry,
no need to sparkle,
no need to be
anyone but oneself.

—Virginia Woolf

You can't be happy without your own permission.

SELF-CONFIDENCE IS THE FIRST REQUISITE TO GREAT UNDERTAKINGS.

-SAMUEL JOHNSON

Be yourself.
No one else
can do it!

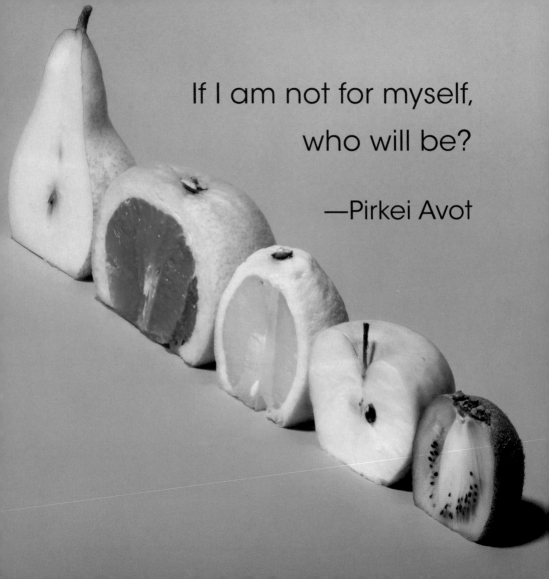

If I am not for myself,
who will be?

—Pirkei Avot

THE IMPORTANT THING IS NOT WHAT THEY THINK OF ME, IT IS WHAT I THINK OF THEM.

– QUEEN VICTORIA

Be thine own palace, or the world's thy jail.

—John Donne

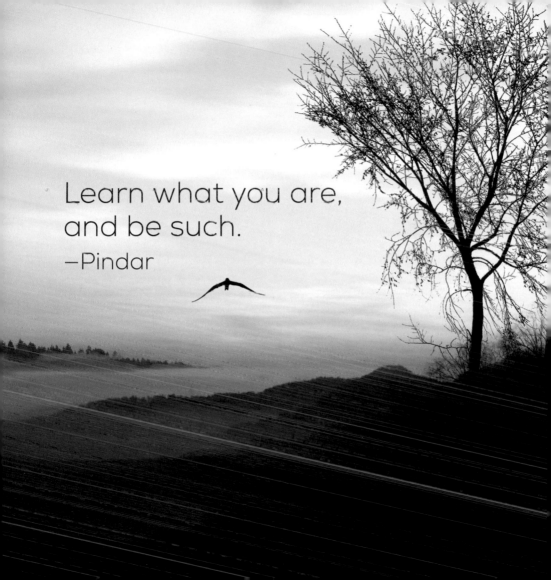

Learn what you are,
and be such.

—Pindar

We must be able to forgive ourselves.

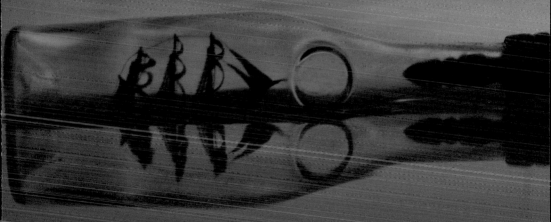

DID ANYONE EVER HAVE A BORING DREAM?

—RALPH HODGSON

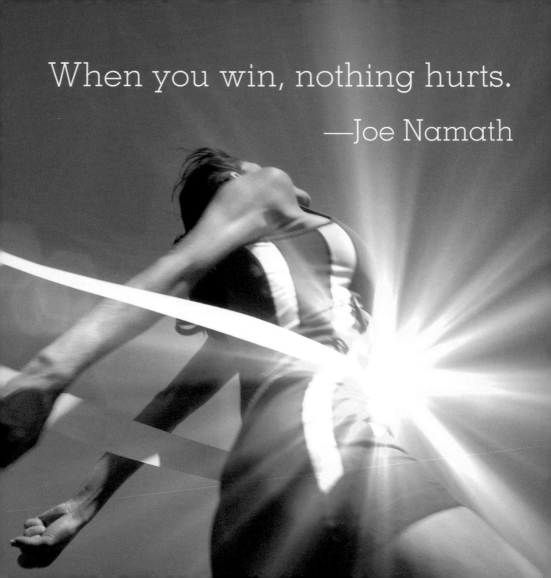

When you win, nothing hurts.

—Joe Namath

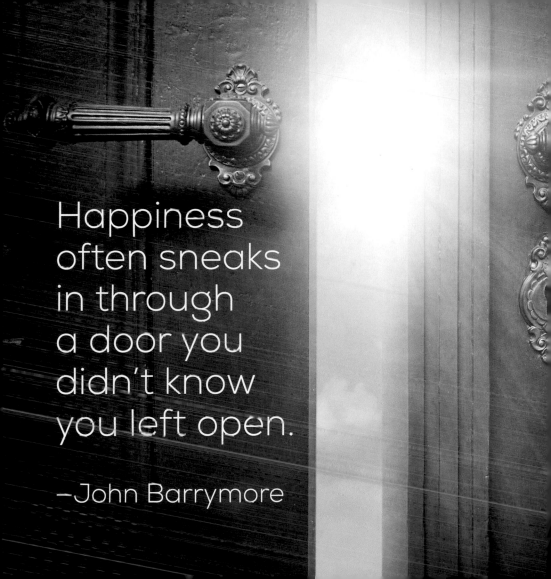

Happiness
often sneaks
in through
a door you
didn't know
you left open.

–John Barrymore

THE GAME ISN'T OVER UNTIL IT'S OVER.
–YOGI BERRA

Progress is a slow process,
but quitting doesn't speed it up.

ONE WHO SPEAKS THE TRUTH IS ALWAYS AT EASE.

—PERSIAN PROVERB

Pretty much all the truth-telling done in the world is done by children.

WITH FREEDOM,
FLOWERS, BOOKS,
AND THE MOON,
WHO COULD NOT
BE PERFECTLY HAPPY?

—OSCAR WILDE

It is better to live rich than to die rich.
—Samuel Johnson

FALL SEVEN TIMES, STAND UP EIGHT.

—JAPANESE PROVERB

DELIBERATE OFTEN — DECIDE ONCE.

-LATIN PROVERB

Although the world is full of suffering, it is full also of the overcoming of it.

—Helen Keller

THE DAYS YOU WORK
ARE THE BEST DAYS.
—GEORGIA O'KEEFFE

Out of the strain of the Doing,
Into the peace of the Done.
—Julia Louise Woodruff

If the only prayer you said in your whole life was "thank you," that would suffice.

–Meister Eckhart

Love yourself first and everything else falls into line. You really have to love yourself to get anything done in this world.

—Lucille Ball

Dwell on the beauty
of life. Watch
the stars, and see
yourself running
with them.
—Marcus Aurelius

YOU NEED TO LET THE LITTLE THINGS THAT WOULD ORDINARILY BORE YOU SUDDENLY THRILL YOU.

—Andy Warhol

THE ONLY WAY ROUND
IS THROUGH.

—ROBERT FROST

EVERYONE MUST ROW WITH THE OARS SHE HAS.

—ENGLISH PROVERB

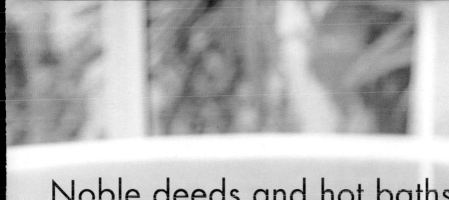

Noble deeds and hot baths are the best cures for depression.

—Dodie Smith

You may be disappointed if you fail, but you are doomed if you don't try.

-Beverly Sills

She who is outside
her door already
has a hard part
of the journey
behind her.
—Dutch proverb

I have an inward
treasure born
within me.
—Charlotte Brontë

BE PATIENT AND TOUGH;
SOMEDAY THIS PAIN WILL
BE USEFUL TO YOU.

-OVID

Don't fight forces;
use them.

—Buckminster Fuller

NOBODY GETS TO LIVE LIFE BACKWARD. LOOK AHEAD, THAT IS WHERE YOUR FUTURE LIES.

—ANN LANDERS

Worries go down better with soup than without.

—Jewish proverb

DON'T WISH AWAY YOUR DAYS, WAITING FOR BETTER ONES AHEAD. THE GRAND AND THE SIMPLE. THEY ARE EQUALLY WONDERFUL.

—MARJORIE PAY HINCKLEY

ACORNS ARE PLANTED SILENTLY BY SOME UNNOTICED BREEZE.

—Thomas Carlyle

In the beginning is my end.
—T. S. Eliot

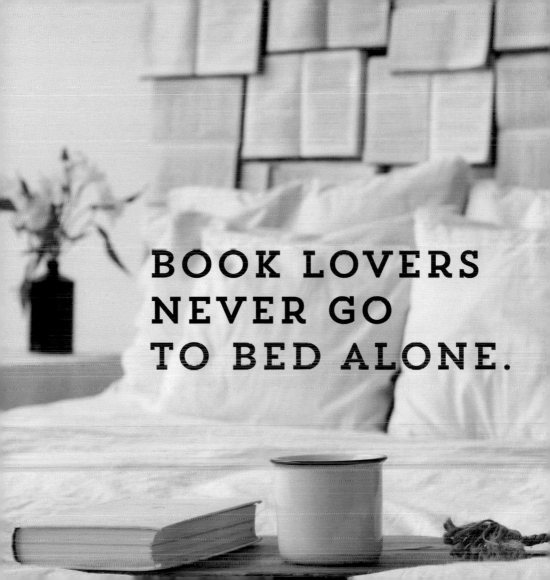

BOOK LOVERS
NEVER GO
TO BED ALONE.

DULLNESS IS
A MISDEMEANOR.
—ETHEL WILSON

And the day came when the risk to remain tight in a bud was more painful than the risk it took to blossom.

—Anaïs Nin

THE HARDER YOU WORK,
THE LUCKIER YOU GET.
—GARY PLAYER

Fortune favors the bold.

—Latin proverb

Luck is being ready
for the chance.
—J. Frank Dobie

SEIZE THE MOMENTS OF HAPPINESS, LOVE AND BE LOVED!

—LEO TOLSTOY

YOU CAN'T STEP INTO THE SAME RIVER TWICE.

-HERACLITUS

We are always the
same age inside.

-Gertrude Stein

TURBULENCE is life force. It is OPPORTUNITY.

—Ramsey Clark

SEEKING MEANS: having a goal. But **FINDING MEANS:** being free, being open, having no goal.

— **HERMANN HESSE**

IF YOU LOOK THE RIGHT WAY, YOU CAN SEE THAT THE WHOLE WORLD IS A GARDEN.

— FRANCES HODGSON BURNETT

Be happy.
It's one way of
being wise.

—Colette

Joy is what happens to us when we allow ourselves to recognize how good things really are.

—Marianne Williamson

The world is full of magic things, patiently waiting for our senses to grow sharper.

—W. B. Yeats

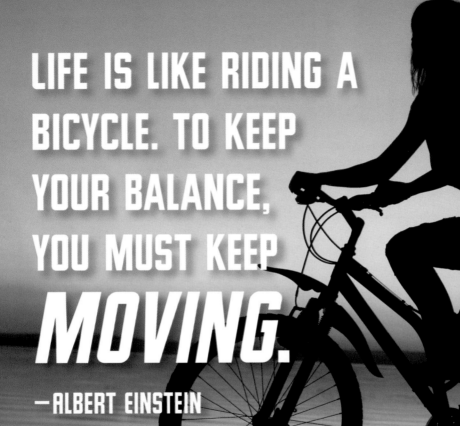

LIFE IS LIKE RIDING A BICYCLE. TO KEEP YOUR BALANCE, YOU MUST KEEP **MOVING.**

—ALBERT EINSTEIN

A truly happy person is one who can enjoy the scenery on the detour.

Nothing is worth more than this day.

—Johann Wolfgang von Goethe

The mere sense of living is joy enough.

—Emily Dickinson

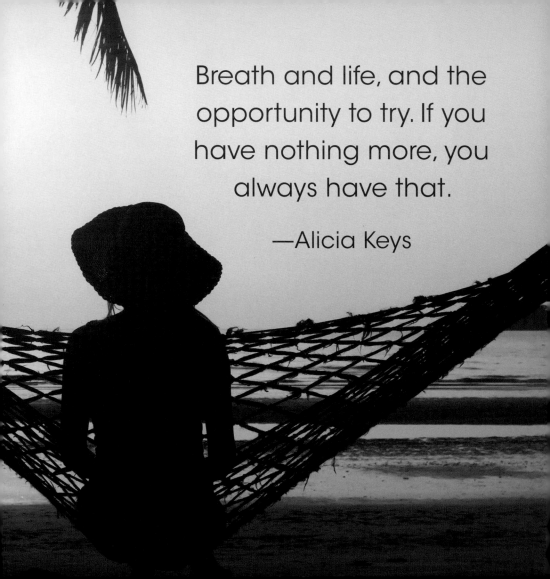

Breath and life, and the opportunity to try. If you have nothing more, you always have that.

—Alicia Keys

Don't look at your feet to see if you are doing it right. Just dance.

—Anne Lamott

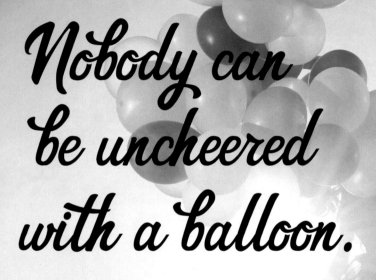

Nobody can
be uncheered
with a balloon.

—A. A. Milne

LIVE IN EACH SEASON AS IT PASSES; BREATHE THE AIR, DRINK THE DRINK, TASTE THE FRUIT, AND RESIGN YOURSELF TO THE INFLUENCES OF EACH.

-HENRY DAVID THOREAU

THINK OF ALL THE BEAUTY THAT'S STILL LEFT IN AND AROUND YOU AND BE HAPPY.

—ANNE FRANK

You are a universe of universes and your soul a source of songs.

—Rubén Dario

JOY DOES NOT SIMPLY
HAPPEN TO US. WE HAVE
TO CHOOSE JOY AND KEEP
CHOOSING IT EVERY DAY.

-HENRI. J. M. NOUWEN

Happiness depends on a good breakfast, flowers in the yard, a drink or a nap.

—Andy Rooney

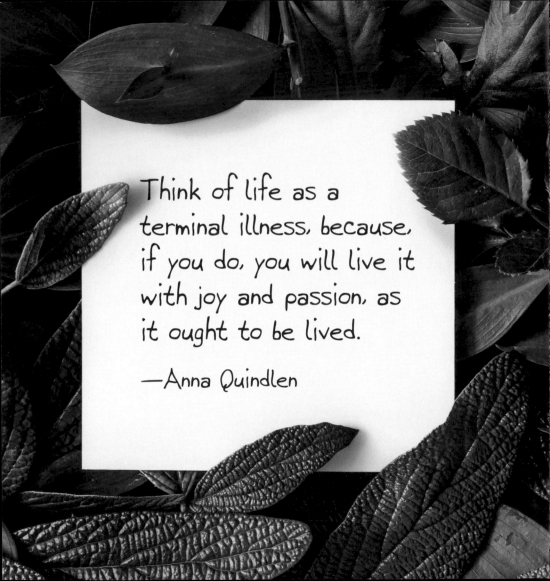

Think of life as a terminal illness, because, if you do, you will live it with joy and passion, as it ought to be lived.

—Anna Quindlen

Rejoice in the things
that are present; all
else is beyond thee.

–Michel Eyquem de Montaigne

WE DON'T KNOW
WHERE WE'RE GOING,
BUT ISN'T IT FUN
TO GO?

-L. M. MONTGOMERY

The sun is always shining someplace.

—Muhammad Ali

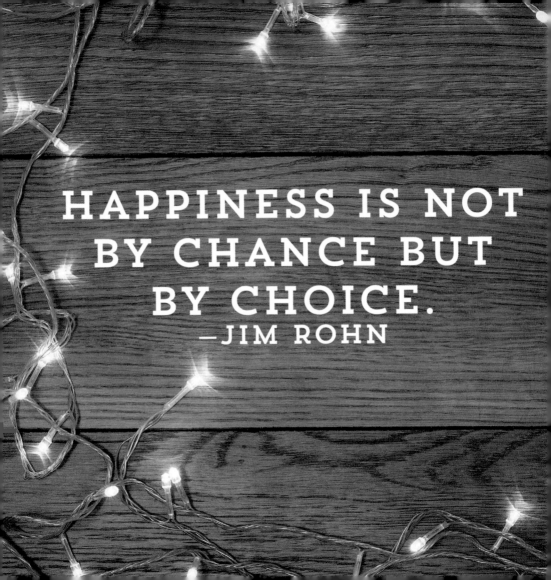

HAPPINESS IS NOT BY CHANCE BUT BY CHOICE.
—JIM ROHN

Seize the moment. Remember all those women on the *Titanic* who waved off the dessert cart.

—Erma Bombeck

Every day is a gift— a new beginning.

—Joye Moon

In spite of
my scars,
I'm tickled
to death
with life!

—Eugene O'Neill

It is no bad thing celebrating a simple life.

—J.R.R. Tolkien

IF WE DON'T LIVE NOW,
WE ARE MISSING LIFE.

-PETRA NĚMCOVÁ

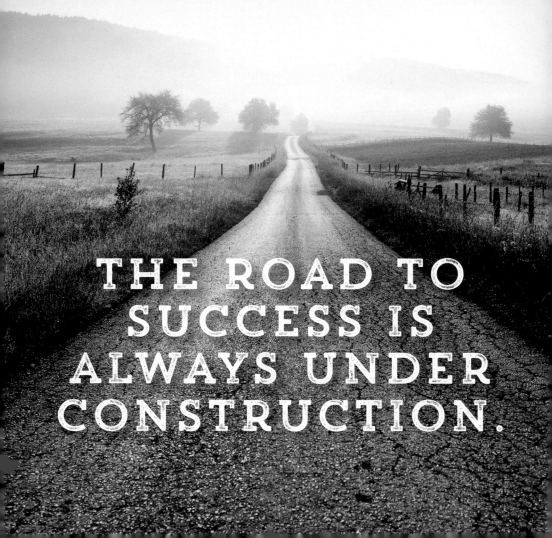

FOR FAST-ACTING RELIEF
TRY SLOWING DOWN.
—LILY TOMLIN

LAUGHTER IS AN INSTANT VACATION.

–MILTON BERLE

DO YOUR THING AND DON'T CARE IF THEY LIKE IT.
—TINA FEY

If you can dance
and be free and
not embarrassed,
you can rule
the world.

—Amy Poehler

Great things never happen in comfort zones.

One small,
positive
thought in the
morning can
change your
whole day.

Life is a beautiful, magnificent thing, even to a jellyfish.

—Charlie Chaplin

One kind word
can warm
three winter
months.

—Japanese proverb

LET YOUR WORK BRAG ABOUT YOU.

Much good work is lost for the lack of a little more.

—E. H. Harriman

Kindness begets kindness.

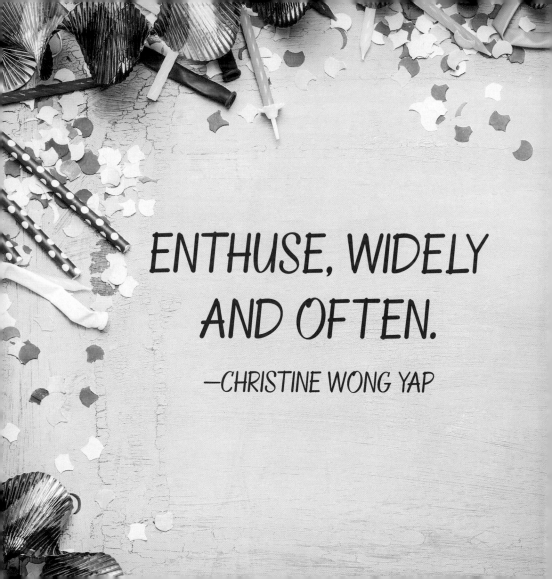

ENTHUSE, WIDELY
AND OFTEN.

—CHRISTINE WONG YAP

FORGIVENESS DOESN'T AVOID PAIN, BUT HEALS IT.

We are all here for a spell, get all the good laughs you can.

—Will Rogers

Talk about your blessings more than you talk about your problems.

Kind words are the music of the world.
-F. W. Faber

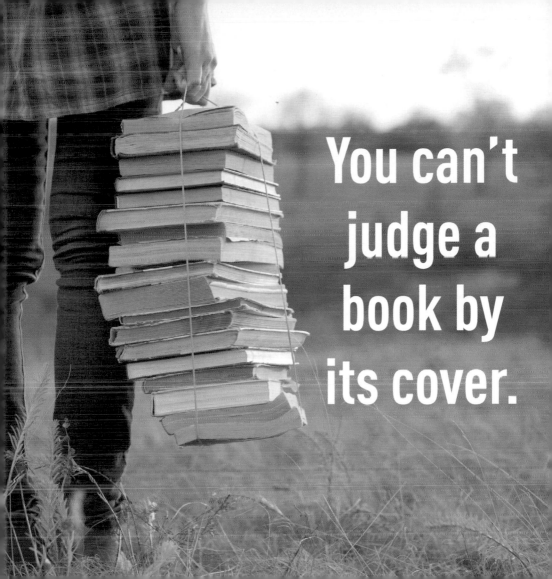

However long the night,
the dawn will break.
—African proverb

DON'T STOP UNTIL YOU'RE PROUD.

The aim of life is to live, and to live means to be aware, joyously, drunkenly, serenely, divinely aware.

—Henry Miller

WHEN YOU FEEL LIKE STOPPING, THINK ABOUT WHY YOU STARTED.

Image Credits

Shutterstock.com: 1 © stockelements; 2, 60, 209 © Jacob_09; 4 © Muhammad Zia; 5 © GaudiLab; 6 © Creativika Graphics; 7 © Evgenii Iaroshevskii; 8 © Masson; 9 © Alexander Mazurkevich; 10 © oatawa; 11 © Guadalupe Polito; 12 © Vikafoto33; 13, 152 © Suzanne Tucker; 14 © Tupungato; 15 © Leonid Ikan; 16 © Galyna Andrushko; 17, 136, 200 © Ditty_about_summer; 18 © Fortyforks; 19 © Lux Blue; 20 © Roop_Dey; 21 © Valentin Agapov; 22, 46, 63, 124, 145 © Floral Deco; 23, 129, 217 © Creative Travel Projects; 24 © Bokeh Blur Background; 25 © Flaffy; 26 © Jag_cz; 27 © tavizta; 28 © Castleski; 29, 72 © Dark Moon Pictures; 30, 198 © nature photos; 31 © Yuganov Konstantin; 32 © stockfotoart; 33 © Elovich; 34 © Annette Shaff; 35 © Monika Wisniewska; 36 © Attitude; 37 © Doidam 10; 38 © Kristina.Co; 39 © fuyu liu; 40 © Dmitry Pichugin; 41 © Cafe Racer; 42 © LittlePerfectStock; 43 © Jenny Sturm; 44 © SimpleThingsHere; 45 © Tom Gowanlock; 47 © Billion Photos; 48 © Chayapol1974; 49 © Nature Bird Photography; 50 © Sunlike; 51 © Grisha Bruev; 52, 156 © jakkapan; 53, 137 © Everett Collection; 54 © REDPIXEL.PL; 55 © Anna Bogush; 56 © anurakss; 57 © Kjpargeter; 58 © JurateBuiviene; 59 © againphoto; 61 © nednapa; 62, 139, 230 © VICUSCHKA; 64 © 24Novembers; 65 © ktsdesign; 66 © UmFOTO; 67 © 578foot; 68 © Rawpixel.com; 69 © CHAINFOTO24; 70 © anakondasp; 71 © Max Topchii; 73, 98, 176 © Africa Studio; 74 © Looker_Studio; 75 © Patrick Thomas; 76 © BABAROGA; 77 © Vasin Lee; 78 © Tono Balaguer; 79 © sniegirova mariia; 80, 220 © Konstanttin; 81 © canadastock; 82 © Rushvol; 83 © bezikus; 84 © travellight; 85, 204, 233 © mythja; 86 © millicookbook; 87 © Erainbow; 88 © oriontrail; 89 © ANEK SANGKAMANEE; 90 © LedyX; 91 © Theeradech Sanin; 92 © Dudarev Mikhail; 93 © Creaturart Images; 94 © THPStock; 95 © everst; 96 © karen roach; 97 © 501room; 99 © Moopixel; 100 © KieferPix; 101 © Patrizia Tilly; 102 © Mirko Macari; 103 © Kotkoa; 104 © Nejron Photo; 105 © Alim Yakubov; 106 © Vitalfoto; 107 © Kris Wiktor; 108 © vvvita; 109 © ShaunWilkinson; 110 © ueuaphoto; 111 © David Porras; 112 © Maria Savenko; 113 © Jason Patrick Ross; 114 © Bernd Schmidt; 115 © Josemaria Toscano; 116 © Mygate; 117, 118 © Triff; 119 © Ioana Catalina E; 120 © Athiyada's; 121 © Rachel Juliet Lerch; 122 © ivantdimov; 123 © Sebastian Knight; 125 © JONATHAN PLEDGER; 126 © Michelle Patrick; 127 © Dave Allen Photography; 128 © encierro; 130, 203 © Gcapture; 131 © Vanillla; 132 © Brandon Bourdages; 133 © Yuliyan Velchev; 134 © jatra; 135 © Paul Aniszewski; 138 © LFP Photography; 140 © iulias; 141 © Sigma_S; 142 © Tomsickova Tatyana; 143 © Vadim Georgiev; 144, 206, 208 © Zamurovic Photography; 146 © Banana Republic images; 147 © Eva Bidiuk; 148 © nguyenkid; 149 © ivantroshka; 150 © sirtravelalot; 151 © Elena Schweitzer; 153 © kathleen collins; 154 © Grzejnik; 155 © Alex Linch; 157 © mdanek; 158 © Photo_DDD; 159 © Markovka; 160 © Leon Aden; 161 © Jurga Jot; 162 © Cecilia Lim H M; 163 © fotogestoeber; 164 © pinkomelet; 165 © Ssokolov; 166 © Trong Nguyen; 167 © Taiga; 168 © Ichiro Murata; 169 © Alena Ozerova; 170 © cagi; 171 © WorldWide; 172 © Brum; 173 © Udo Kieslich; 174 © Onishchenko Natalya; 175 © Melissa King; 177 © Ttstudio; 178 © fabiodevilla; 179 © Kasabutskaya Nataliya; 180 © Anders Ipsen; 181 © gkondratenko; 182 © Mila_1989; 183 © lithian; 184 © imacoconut; 185 © Uhryn Larysa; 186 © Pitipat Usanakornkul; 187 © Drepicter; 188 © Petar Bogdanov; 189 © NCG PHOTOGRAPHY; 190 © J. Lekavicius; 191 © Wichukorn Nilmanat; 192 © Oleg Znamenskiy; 193 © Dennis Jacobsen; 194 © Nopparat Promtha; 195 © Siriwadee maplook jeab; 196 © maradon 333; 197 © GoldenStar - FOTOGRAFIE; 199 © BUNDITINAY; 201 © ayarx oren; 202 © Kuznetcov_Konstantin; 205 © Stefano Garau; 207, 216 © Julia Sudnitskaya; 210 © Evgeniia Freeman; 211 © stockphoto mania; 212 © Marko Aliaksandr; 213 © Katerina Andreeva; 214 © mama_mia; 215 © PopTika; 218 © Weston; 219 © YIUCHEUNG; 221 © Tonko Oosterink; 222 © tomertu; 223 © MaxyM; 224 © wk1003mike; 225 © Olena Kibryk; 226 © Mila Drumeva; 227 © Hafiez Razali; 228 © Alina G; 229 © Anton_Ivanov; 231 © Amy Christenson; 232 © Irina Kozorog; 234 © Zacky24; 235 © Rasstock; 236 © Peter Wollinga; 237 © Sweet Art; 238 © Olesya Kuznetsova; 239 © zhukovvvlad; 240 © Ratana21